The Gift of
Everything

Also by Lang Leav

FICTION
Sad Girls
Poemsia

POETRY
Love & Misadventure
Lullabies
Memories
The Universe of Us
Sea of Strangers
Love Looks Pretty on You
September Love

The Gift of Everything

Lang Leav

Andrews McMeel
PUBLISHING®

Andrews McMeel Publishing
a division of Andrews McMeel Universal
1130 Walnut Street, Kansas City, Missouri 64106

www.andrewsmcmeel.com

21 22 23 24 25 SDB 10 9 8 7 6 5 4 3 2 1

ISBN: 978-1-5248-6886-4

Library of Congress Control Number: 2021939890

Editor: Patty Rice
Art Director/Designer: Diane Marsh
Production Editor: Dave Shaw
Production Manager: Cliff Koehler

ATTENTION: SCHOOLS AND BUSINESSES
Andrews McMeel books are available at quantity discounts with bulk purchase for educational, business, or sales promotional use. For information, please e-mail the Andrews McMeel Publishing Special Sales Department: specialsales@amuniversal.com.

For my readers.

You have been the greatest gift of all.

Introduction

As I was putting together this collection, there was a sense that I was not only revisiting my past, but also taking parts of it with me into the present. In doing so, I felt a wonderful completeness to this book.

Time has never felt linear to me. Conversations that happened years ago seem more vivid and present than the ones I've had just days before, which is why I have chosen to intersperse the thirty-five new poems throughout this collection like stars scattered across the night sky. I felt their natural place was with their predecessors and it would be a poetic and fluid way to present this anthology.

The Gift of Everything celebrates the past decade of my life, marking the pivotal moment I shared my first poem, "Sea of Strangers," on Tumblr to seeing through a long-cherished dream of having my poetry read and loved by so many. Going further back, *The Gift of Everything* is a nod to my childhood, where my poetry-filled notebooks were circulating around the schoolyard.

As poets, we are constantly collaborating with our past selves—it is only through our memories that we are able to become fully formed in the present. We never truly know when something will end. But beginnings are much easier to recognize, which is why I feel it is befitting to leave you with a poem I wrote as an eleven-year-old girl, on the first page of what was perhaps my first-ever anthology:

A glimpse through these pages
Is a journey through my heart
So turn this page my friend
And let your journey start

Much love, Lang

FINIS CORONAT OPUS

1 Old Love

I don't know what I'd say to you now.

Now the words that have once flowed so readily for you are running dry.

I guess I could tell you that I've stopped checking my horoscope. I guess I would say I've stopped reading yours. I've stopped looking you up.

I'd always imagined we'd stay exactly as we were. But time is cruel, and we gave up so much for others who wouldn't have done the same for us.

I guess love does get old, same as everything else. It just takes a little longer.

2 **My Mother**

My mother was a woman
without country as I lay
curled in her womb

Her body marked for death
teeming with life. My life
barely a glow when she
glared into the pit of darkness
a hairline crack from death
crawling to the light
dreaming of a faraway shore
and a little girl in her arms

My mother, my safe passage
into this world, fought a war
to show me wars can be won

3 **The Edge of the World**

You think falling in love is about holding on, but it isn't. It is hands gripping the edge of the world and letting go, one finger at a time.

Take a deep breath—here comes the drop. I know it's your first time here, but soon you will get used to the motion; the headlong dive into the deep.

Just go with it.

You only get one chance to fall in love with your heart still whole.

4 **Time**

You were the one
I wanted most
to stay

But time could not
be kept at bay

The more it goes
the more it's gone—
the more it takes away

5 **To Love You**

It feels bittersweet to love you, as though time has already run its ruinous path and everything good is over before it begins.

It feels perilous to love you, like a dust storm swallowing up the sky or a comet skimming the stratosphere.

But it is an honor to love you. I will love you for as long as I can.

6 **Over**

It's over, she said.

It was many years later when the quiet realization dawned on her.

It's over, her heart whispered.

7 **Dear February**

You were always the month of goodbyes
standing sentry to autumn and her changing hues
Tall trees and dappled light on the city pavement
shifting under my feet, skirting the cracks
I think of my mother and what she lost one February
and there are things you know about me
that I don't want her to know
Is my secret safe with you, dear February?
Like you I am caught between the city lights and the sea
torn between my love and my home
Like you I am the sun that keeps setting too soon
missing the summer even while I'm here

8 **Anxiety**

I struggle with things that are as easy to others as breathing. Like breathing. Like answering the phone. Or sending that email I have been meaning to for weeks. I panic when I am asked out to dinner, even if it's with someone I really want to see. It's hard for me to commit to anything, and when I do, I overthink it until my brain tells me I have made a mistake, like a rat caught in a maze, trying to claw its way out.

I don't know why I am like this. People ask me why I can't do anything without jumping through a thousand thoughts, like hoops. But sometimes I wonder if my inability to function in the real world is really such a bad thing. I wonder if that's why I've spent so much time sheltered in my imagination.

And because I can't live in the real world, I create worlds to belong to. And I wonder if the very thing I've always been told is my weakness has, all along, been my strength.

9 **Writing**

There is one thing you should know about writing. It will inevitably lead you to dark places, as you cannot write authentically about something unless you have lived it.

However, you should always bear in mind that you are only a tourist and must always remain one. You were meant to use your gift with words to bring a voice to suffering. But do not be too indulgent despite how addictive sadness can be, how easy it is to get lost down the path of self-destruction. You must emerge from adversity, scathed but victorious to tell your story and, in turn, light the way for others.

10 **A Time Line**

You and I
against a rule
set for us by time

A marker drawn
to show our end
etched into its line

The briefest moment
shared with you—
the longest
on my mind

11 **My Life**

I will celebrate this life of mine, with or without you. The moon does not need the sun to tell her she is whole.

12 **The Loneliest Place**

I believe there is penance in yearning. There is poverty in giving away too much of your heart. When the desire for another is not returned in equal measure—nothing in the world could compensate for the shortfall.

Sometimes the loneliest place to be is in love.

13 **To Myself, Ten Years Ago**

You won't believe what I see from this vantage point, the years stretching out before you like a long and winding road. I don't want to scare you, but there is a forest just up ahead. One so dense and dark, the sunlight won't reach you for a while. You will wander lost, in this long, perilous night, not knowing if it will ever come to an end. But believe me, the light will find you again, and when it does, you will no longer be afraid of the dark.

Stop to catch your breath. Soon, a jagged mountain will rise before you, so steep it will make you want to turn back around. Don't despair; the first foothold is always the most difficult and every inch you claim of that cold, hard precipice will make you stronger. Before you know it, the ground will level out beneath you, and you will look back to see you had conquered what you once thought impossible.

See that turn just up ahead? That's the place where love will meet you, with arms so warm it will melt away the winter in an instant. And then, it will be summer for a very long time.

14 **Crossroads**

It was a quiet love, a tacit love. It came without prelude or preamble. We never said the word love—we didn't have to. It was in our laughter, in the sense of wonder we found in each other. And if we had doubts then, time has told us otherwise.

It was a gentle love, a tactile love. It was all hands and lips and hearts in tandem. There was motion in our bodies and emotion in our discourse. We were a symphony of melody and melancholy. When you find peace in another's presence, there is no mistaking.

It was a kind love, a selfless love. I was a dreamer, and you were a traveler. We met at the crossroads. I saw love in your smile and recognized it for the first time in my life. But you had a plane to catch, and I was already home.

15 **A Woman**

The day you become a woman, they hand you a grenade. And you must choose between hurling or holding. Between want and expectation. Excise your desire, while you are hungry for everything. Give up your life for a version of you that isn't you at all.

Do not think twice about the imposition when they tell you, there is nothing worse than a fallen woman. Nothing worse than a woman who doesn't know her place. You will learn otherwise when you trade your truth for an ideal that no amount of good you do will ever be enough anyway.

So, make up your own rules. Don't be afraid to hurl, to fall, to get dirt on your face. Sweetheart, let this be your one glorious mess because in the end the only person you should answer to is yourself.

After all, *you are a woman,*

And long before they punish you for what you've done, they will punish you for what you are.

16 Division

We inhabit the same world
but do not share a common reality.

17 **I Should Have Left You Then**

In the glow of my eternal youth
when I had yet to learn my truth
in sun-soaked days I saw no end—
I should have left you then

When my life felt like it wasn't mine
and I knew I was running out of time
that if I didn't leave, I'd never know—
I should have let you go

When the world had yet its fill of me
and there was so much left to see
my love, I should have left you when
there was time for me to start again

18 **A Dream**

As the Earth began spinning faster and faster, we floated upward, hands locked tightly together, eyes sad and bewildered. We watched as our faces grew younger and realized the Earth was spinning in reverse, moving us backward in time.

Then we reached a point where I no longer knew who you were, and I was grasping the hands of a stranger. But I didn't let go. And neither did you.

I had my first dream about you last night.
She smiles. Really? What was it about?
I don't remember exactly, but the whole time I was dreaming, I knew you were mine.

19 **Wallflower**

Shrinking in a corner
pressed into the wall
do they know I'm present
am I here at all?

Is there a written rule book
that tells you how to be
all the right things to talk about
that everyone has but me

Slowly I am withering—
a flower deprived of sun
longing to belong to—
somewhere or someone

20 **To Yourself**

Pick yourself up. Get it together. Not because others have it worse than you. Not because you owe it to anyone to put on a smile. But because you have your mother's blood flowing through your veins. And even if you think otherwise, you matter to so many people. But first of all, you need to matter to yourself.

21 **Poetry**

I know you have seen things you wish you hadn't. You have done things you wish you could take back. And you wonder why you were thrown into the thick of it all—why you had to suffer the way you did. And as you are sitting there alone and hurting, I wish I could put a pen in your hand and gently remind you how the world has given you poetry and now you must give it back.

22 **Déjà Vu**

I saw it once
I have no doubt
but now can't place
its whereabouts

I try to think it
time and time
but what it is
won't come to mind

A word, a scent—
a feeling, past
It will not show
though much I've asked

And when it comes
I soon forget—
this is how it felt
when we first met

23 **Rogue Planets**

As a kid, I would count backward from ten and imagine at one, there would be an explosion—perhaps caused by a rogue planet crashing into Earth or some other major catastrophe. When nothing happened, I'd feel relieved and at the same time, a little disappointed.

I think of you at ten; the first time I saw you. Your smile at nine and how it lit up something inside me I had thought long dead. Your lips at eight pressed against mine and at seven, your warm breath in my ear and your hands everywhere. You tell me you love me at six and at five we have our first real fight. At four we have our second and three, our third. At two you tell me you can't go on any longer and then at one, you ask me to stay.

And I am relieved, so relieved—and a little disappointed.

24 **Lost and Found**

A sunken chest
on the ocean ground
to never be found
was where he found me

There he stirred
my every thought
my every word
so gently, so profoundly

Now I am kept
from dreams I dreamt
when once I slept
so soundly

25 Sydney, 2007

Today I saw a photograph of the Argyle tunnel, projected with light, blooming with flowers, and it brought back a decade-old memory.

I was young and broken. But hopeful.

I was alone as I walked through the tunnel, my keys splayed between the fingers of my clenched fist in a makeshift weapon. I was thinking, I should have left the party earlier. I was thinking, I should have asked someone to walk me to my car. I was thinking of the long drive ahead. I was thinking of the porch light my mother always left on for me.

As that girl, I couldn't see the future ahead. As the woman now, I can see it all. The pitfalls, the tragedies, the near misses and close calls, the years of wanting, waiting, wishing. The agony and beauty of my strange and twisted path.

I can see it all for her, as she is walking through that tunnel, not knowing what is waiting for her on the other side. I wish I could tell her that we made it home.

26 **You Had Me Once**

You had me once—
wild and willing
you wanted a lover
who took you to the edge

Wasn't it I—
who gave you that feeling?
A love that danced
upon a ledge

Then came another
who offered you shelter—
and you chose to be
with her instead

27 **To Get Here**

You and your endearing quirks—the curious tilt of your head—that adorable twitch at the corner of your mouth when you're on the verge of laughter. You, with your hand clasped in mine, throwing backward glances at the three-quarter moon as we stumble down side streets guided by paper lanterns expecting some grand adventure while every new thing you say spins us into a whole other world. How did I find you in all this mess? And aren't you always saying how glad you are to have met me? It seems like everywhere else was a place we had to go through to get here. And I love you so much—too much. If ever there was such a thing.

28 **I Know Love**

I know love now because I am in love. Because of how long I've loved. Because of the man I love.

Love used to be a beautiful mirage, a moonbeam on the water I tried to cup in my hands. Now it is a grand oak tree, tried and tested, roots driving deep down into the earth.

I have a love that takes me across oceans. A love that tells me I am home, no matter where I am in the world.

29 **Sea of Strangers**

In a sea of strangers
you've longed to know me
Your life spent sailing
to my shores

The arms that yearn
to someday hold me
will ache beneath
the heavy oars

Please take your time
and take it slowly
as all you do
will run its course

And nothing else
can take what only—
was always meant
as solely yours

30 **No Other**

There is someone I keep in my heart—I love him and no one else. It is a love that will only die with me.

You may ask, death could be some time away—what if from now to then, you love someone new?

Well, I can tell you, there is only one love. If any person claims to have loved twice in all their life—they have not loved at all.

31 **Vultures**

We all have moments of darkness, moments when we are so unlike ourselves. And like vultures they wait for a slip, a misstep, then they take that part of us and try to convince the world that is all we are.

32 **I Loved Him**

I loved how his eyes danced merrily
and the gentle way he spoke
the way he filled my aimless days
with bitterness and hope

I loved him as I fell to sleep
and each morning as I woke
I loved him with all my wayward heart—
until the day it broke

33 **Procession**

He used to ask me all the time if I was okay. As though he never knew for sure. He would ask me when he was tired or frustrated or when he felt helpless. He would ask me when he was afraid.

He asked me that same question, long after we stopped being lovers—when we became something less yet somehow more.

Are you okay? He would whisper on the phone late at night, when his girlfriend was asleep or had gone to her mother's for the weekend. *Are you okay?*

He hasn't asked me in years, but I know he still thinks it. I know the question still reverberates in his mind like a broken record and he will keep looking for answers long after there is nothing left to appease him.

It was always the same question, over and over. Like the start of a procession. And it took me years to recognize the unsaid words that marched silently behind.

Are you okay; *because I love you.*
Are you okay; *because I need you.*
Are you okay; *because I don't know how to live without you.*

34 **Every Other Girl**

There is me and there is every other girl. And you still can't decide between the two.

35 **Moment of Truth**

One day I looked at you and it occurred to me how beautiful your smile was. I heard music in your laughter—I saw poetry in your words. You asked me why I had that look on my face, as though a shadow had fallen across its sun-drenched landscape, heavy with premonition, dark with revelation.

The second I tried to tell myself I wasn't in love was the moment I realized I was.

36 **All I Want**

I'm not asking for a grand declaration of love. I've stopped entertaining those thoughts long ago. You see, I have resigned myself to where I am now, hanging by a thin, tenuous thread. I can feel it twisting above me, gently fraying, slowly giving way. I'm not asking for promises or tenure—I just want a hand to reach for at the breaking point.

37 **Soul Mates**

I don't know how you are so familiar to me—or why it feels less like I am getting to know you and more as though I am remembering who you are. How every smile, every whisper brings me closer to the impossible conclusion that I have known you before, I have loved you before—in another time, a different place—some other existence.

38 **Broken Hearts**

I know you've lost someone and it hurts. You may have lost them suddenly, unexpectedly. Or perhaps you began losing pieces of them until one day, there was nothing left. You may have known them all your life or you may have barely known them at all. Either way, it is irrelevant—you cannot control the depth of a wound another inflicts upon you.

Which is why I am not here to tell you tomorrow will be a new day. That the sun will go on shining. Or there are plenty of fish in the sea. What I will tell you is this; it's okay to be hurting as much as you are. What you are feeling is not only completely valid but necessary—because it makes you so much more human. And though I can't promise it will get better any time soon, I can tell you that it will—eventually. For now, all you can do is take your time. Take all the time you need.

39 **Self-Love**

Once when I was running
from all that haunted me
to the dark I was succumbing—
to what hurt unbearably

Searching for the one thing
that would set my sad soul free

In time I stumbled upon it
an inner calm and peace
and now I am beginning
to see and to believe
in who I am becoming—
and all I've yet to be

40 Beautiful Things

They say you're overly sensitive. That your heart sits too comfortably at the precipice, ready to plummet at the slightest provocation. An unkind word can send you spiraling. A perceived indifference shakes you down to your core. You don't know why you absorb feelings so readily, even when they aren't your own. But one day, you will learn to appreciate the gift you have been given. To live in peace with your sentimentality and, from this raw and tender place, create the most beautiful things.

41 **Closure**

Like time suspended
a wound unmended—
you and I

We had no ending
no said goodbye

For all my life
I'll wonder why

42 No Longer Mine

It should be my right to mourn someone who has yet to leave this world but no longer wants to be part of mine.

43 **Angels**

It happens like this. One day you meet someone and for some inexplicable reason, you feel more connected to this stranger than anyone else—closer to them than your closest family.

Perhaps because this person carries an angel within them—one sent to you for some higher purpose, to teach you an important lesson or to keep you safe during a perilous time. What you must do is trust in them—even if they come hand in hand with pain or suffering—the reason for their presence will become clear in due time.

Though here is a word of warning—you may grow to love this person but remember they are not yours to keep. Their purpose isn't to save you but to show you how to save yourself. And once this is fulfilled, the halo lifts and the angel leaves their body as the person exits your life. They will be a stranger to you once more.

It's so dark right now, I can't see any light around me. That's because the light is coming from you. You can't see it but everyone else can.

44 **From You**

The distance from you is measured in how far I've come.

45 **Lullabies**

I barely know you, she says, voice heavy with sleep. I don't know your favorite color or how you like your coffee. What keeps you up at night or the lullabies that sing you to sleep. I don't know a thing about the first girl you loved, why you stopped loving her or why you still do.

I don't know how many millions of cells you are made of and if they have any idea they are part of something so beautiful and unimaginably perfect.

I may not have a clue about any of these things, but this— she places her hand on his chest—this I know.

46 **Punished**

"We were happy," she said, and her eyes, downcast and brimming, reminded him of how the sky was before the first splash of rain.

"We were happy, and they punished us for it."

47 **The Narcissist**

Writers fall in love like anyone else
Lovers want to be their muse
He said, *If I broke your heart*
would you write about me?

And then he did it
just to see what I would do

48 **The Redwood Tree**

My father once told me a story about an old redwood tree—how she stood tall and proud—her sprawling limbs clothed in emerald-green. With a smile, he described her as a mere sapling, sheltered by her elders and basking in the safety of the warm, dappled light. But as this tree grew taller, she found herself at the mercy of the cruel wind and the vicious rain. Together, they tore at her pretty boughs until she felt as though her heart would split in two.

After a long, thoughtful pause, my father turned to me and said, My daughter, one day the same thing will happen to you. And when that time comes, remember the redwood tree. Do not worry about the cruel wind or the vicious rain—but do as that tree did and just keep growing.

49 **After All**

I felt you again in my sleep last night. Like always my dreams of you are peripheral. An overheard conversation where your name is mentioned; a letter in my hand I try desperately to read before I wake. A Styrofoam coffee cup and half-read book on an empty table where I knew you were just minutes before. It's as though my dreams are a mirror of my waking world, like finding myself walking down the street where I could have sworn I caught a glimpse of you, only to look again and realize it wasn't you after all.

50 **How Little**

How deeply you have hurt me. How oblivious you are to the fact. It's as though we speak a different language. Like you do not hear a thing I say. Or perhaps you choose not to. Don't you know how little it takes to assuage me?

How easy it is for you to make me happy?

How sad it is you won't.

51 **Your Life**

You've wandered off too far
you've forgotten who you are
you've let down the ones you love
you've given up too much

You once made a deal with time
but it's slipping by too fast
you can't borrow from the future
to make up for the past

You forsake all that you hold dear
for a dream that is not your own
you would rather live a lie—
than live your life alone

52 **The One Thing**

Look at you. You've stitched your life so perfectly together. You've worked so damn hard to get to where you are, and now have everything you want.

So why do you keep looking back at the one thing that can undo it all?

53 **The Perfect Crime**

It wasn't with knives
my heart he tore
when he brought me
to death's door

It wasn't his hands
that had me slain—
but he had killed me
all the same

Cold and callous
with no remorse
he turned me to
a walking corpse

And I—imprisoned
in this pain
while he without
the slightest blame—
free to do it
over again

54 **Today**

Today I am not in my skin. My body cannot contain me. I am spilling out and over, like a rogue wave on the shore. Today I can't keep myself from feeling like I don't have a friend in the world. And no matter how hard I try, I can't seem to pick myself up off the floor. My demons are lying in wait, they are grinning in the shadows, their polished fangs glinting, knowing today, it will be an easy kill. But tomorrow, tomorrow could be different, and that is what keeps me going today.

55 **Night Drives**

The day had started late
And now it's one a.m.
Like the closing of a gate
The night soon gone again

When we lose the ones we love
There is no one left to blame
Like a journey with no direction
A road without a name

But there's no point in turning back
I'm stuck in this one-way lane
Where the waiting drives me mad
And the hoping keeps me sane

56 **Sunday Best**

Do you remember that night I turned up on your doorstep? I was wearing my Sunday best. You watched the mascara as it ran down like fault lines, and you knew I had blood on my lips.

I'm tired of running, I said—
and the earth shook a little

So am I, you replied
as it shook a little more
I don't want anyone else, I whispered
And I felt myself crumble.

You held out your arms and I was cracked porcelain. We looked at each other as we stood at the precipice. And I knew once I fell, I'd never stop falling. And everything before you would be time to kill. You said you were scared but you couldn't ignore it.

And that was the moment when we became real.

57 **Façade**

Do you believe in fairy tales?
My once upon a time
my read between the lines

My ordinary, everyday
do you need another rhyme?
Am I just an old cliché

Did I take a wrong turn somewhere
got lost along the way
Did a year pass by each day?

You haven't asked me for some time
if I am doing fine
As long as I tack on this smile

And never show you the face behind
or tell you what's been on my mind
We can stay like this awhile

58 **The Rose**

Have you ever loved a rose
and watched her slowly bloom
and as her petals would unfold
you grew drunk on her perfume

Have you ever seen her dance
her leaves all wet with dew
and quivered with a new romance—
the wind, he loved her too

Have you ever longed for her
on nights that go on and on
for now, her face is all a blur
like a memory kept too long

Have you ever loved a rose
and bled against her thorns
and swear each night to let her go
then love her more by dawn

59 **Letter to the Past**

Tomorrow, you're going to fall in love, and it won't be pretty. Tell your mother, even though it will terrify her. Tell her you love him so much, that for once in your life, you don't have words for it. Tell her it hurts when he looks at you, when he takes from you. Tell her how the sun has betrayed you, how she only carries his light. When he isn't there, everything is a shadow of his absence.

Don't go upstairs with him. You're going to regret it. He'll never change. I know you're so lonely you can't stand it. The kind of lonely that has teeth. A lone wolf howling at the moon. There is a savagery to what you feel. It eats you up inside. But you will get through it; you don't need his mouth to placate you. You don't need his hands to untangle the butterfly knot in your heart. Your love is a fire that will burn itself out. Let it ravage you.

Things are coming you can't even imagine. If you knew what they were, you would forgive this one injustice, this one catastrophe that has brought your life to a screeching, screaming halt. The world will turn for you again, and when it does, it will take you anywhere you want.

I have to go now, but I love you. I need to leave you, but I'll always be with you. One day, you'll meet me here, and I will tell you this: I will tell you that we made it.

60 **My Own Self**

Everything I write is observational—even when it is my own self I am watching.

61 **All or Nothing**

If you love me
for what you see
only your eyes would be
in love with me

If you love me
for what you've heard
then you would love me
for my words

If you love
my heart and mind
then you would love me
for all that I'm

But if you don't love
my every flaw
then you mustn't love me—
not at all

62 **At Last**

Love looks pretty on you. Makes you soft, tender, proud. Makes you sit up and take notice. Gives you a home to set down your things.

What a blessing it is, to have music and dancing and poetry. What a gift it is, to look at someone and say, I'm so happy to have found you—at last, at last, at long, long last—you're here.

63 **A Lesson**

There is a girl who smiles all the time
to show the world that she is fine
A boy who surrounds himself with friends
wishes that his life would end

For those that say they never knew—
the saddest leave the least of clues

64 **Wild Thing**

It's been awhile since I was a wild thing. Now in my natural habitat, I have come into my own

Let my hair engulf my crown like a darkening sky, swallowing the sun, leaving specks of gold like stars by night

Let my nails lengthen, harden, sharpen into spikes

My mother once told me tales of wolves, to keep my storybook body safe—a body I have since let go to ruin, let soften and settle like an old, abandoned house, surrendered like a breath let out

I was curved to fit the shape of someone's mouth, and I shut my own against the false narrative,

Let them have their way—I say

I'm a wild thing again today

In my long season of silence, I have met with the darkest part of myself, and I am no longer, no longer afraid

65 **Poetry and Prose**

Sometimes I am caught between poetry and prose, like two lovers I can't decide between.

Prose says to me, let's build something long and lasting.

Poetry takes me by the hand, and whispers, *Come with me, let's get lost for a while.*

66 **An Artist in Love**

I drew him in my world
I write him in my lines
I want to be his girl
he was never meant as mine

I drew him in my world
he is always on my mind
I draw his every line
It hurts when he's unkind

I drew him in my world
I draw him all the time
but I don't know where
to draw the line

67 **September Love**

How many years must we put between us to prove we are no longer in love? How many summers and Septembers, distractions and chance meetings, remnants of our sad, hopeful love in another's look, an all too familiar gesture—how long do we go on dragging our bodies day after day through this yawning, yearning world, searching for a glimpse of what could have been?

Tell me there has been someone else like me, for you. That your experience of love has not been defined by the way I spoke your name into the hollow of your neck. Ask me if I have found the same kind of reverence anywhere else but in your slow, patient hands, your sea-salt lips spilling laughter mid-sentence, my heart rising in a crescendo like a wave ready to crash.

As you whispered to me, *Love is the only thing that time cannot touch.*

After all this time, my love for you burns constant and true, my guiding light, my morning star. Time is testament to the relentless, unyielding power of this old, ancient love. A love I will carry with me, from eons to oceans to inches, back to you.

68 **Her**

There is so much history in the way he looks at her. In the way he says her name. Whenever they meet, there is a current that runs between them like an electric charge on the verge of erupting into a perfect storm.

I don't love her anymore, he says.

And it is in the way he says the word *her*—that tells me otherwise.

69 **The End**

I don't know what to say, he said
It's okay, she replied, I know what we are—
and I know what we're not

70 **Missing Parts**

There is so much beauty in not getting what you want. So much creation and art. You'd think that the universe withholds from you, just so it can witness what you will do with your longing; how you will fill in the missing parts.

71 **Numbers**

Nothing felt like mine anymore, not after you. All those little things that defined me; small sentimental trinkets, car keys, pin codes, and passwords. They all felt like you. And more than anything else, my number—the one you boldly asked for that night, amidst a sea of people, under a sky of talking satellites and glowing stars.

You said no matter how many times you erased me from your phone, you would still recognize that number when it flashed on your screen. The series of sixes and nines, like the dip of my waist to the curve of my hips, your hands pressed into the small of my back. Nines and sixes that were reminiscent of two contented cats, curled together like a pair of speech marks. You said if you could never hold me or kiss me again, you could live with that. But you couldn't bear the thought of us not speaking and asked, at the very least, could I just allow you that one thing?

I wonder what went through your mind the day you dialed my number to find it had been disconnected. If your imagination had raced with thoughts of what new city I had run to and who was sharing my bed. Isn't it strange how much of our lives are interchangeable, how little is truly ours? Someone else's ringtone, someone else's song, someone else's words, someone else's broken heart. These are the things we inherit by choice or by chance.

And it wasn't my choice to love you but it was mine to leave. I don't think the moon ever meant to be a satellite, kept in loving orbit, locked in hopeless inertia, destined to repeat the same pattern over and over—to meet in eclipse with the sun—only when the numbers allowed.

72 Where You Are Loved

Don't stay where you are needed. Go where you are loved.

73 **Revenge**

When the battle is done
and you think you have won—
don't dance on my grave just yet

If you are the moon
then I am the sun—
I will not allow you to forget

In my own time
I will take back what's mine
for I am not your friend

In the dark of the night
And the shifting of tides—
I will come for you then

74 **Ten Things**

There came a time when you were allowed only ten
worldly possessions

Down by my feet were the things I had chosen

The first was a clock to tell the time. And to feel a
heartbeat that was separate to mine

A pencil, eraser, and book of blank pages, words written
on sand through all the ages

A spoon and bowl my fifth and sixth, a phantom meal for
me to lick

My seventh a cup to catch the rain, to quench my thirst
and dull my pain

A pillow in the place of my bed, to rest my head

My ninth, a quilt against the cold, something to hold

And when I was down to one, I couldn't choose

between a knife and a picture of you

75 **Us**

I love him and he loves me.

We spend every moment together. When sleep parts us, we often meet in our dreams.

I like to take naps throughout the day. Like a cat, he says. He is a cat person.

He thinks my eyes are beautiful and strange. He has never seen eyes like mine up close before. He says they look at him with daggers when he has done something wrong. Like when he forgets to order olives on my half of the pizza.

He thinks I am especially cute when angry.

We argue over whose turn it is to put the DVD in the player.

Sometimes no one wins and we end up watching bad TV.

Which is never really a bad thing.

He never imagined he would be with someone like me.

Now, he says, he can't imagine himself with anyone else.

∽

We're kids, aren't we?
Yes, kids with grown-up powers.

76 **More or Less**

When love is seen
from two points of view
what we were
I can only guess

I am certain it was love
with you—
but to love
you did not confess

So was it I—
who made it more?
Or was it you—
who made it less?

77 **House of Straw**

Women, build your house while you are young. When your shoulders can carry the world. Before the weight of children and men. Build your house. Not with needles and haystacks. Not with wood and sticks. Not with matches and straw. Build your house with bricks.

Protect yourself from the wind and the wolves. Arm yourself with nails. Paper and pen. Hang your name on your door. Only then are you safe in the house of bricks you've built, when this house you've built is yours.

78 **Until It's Gone**

Some people don't know what they have until it's gone.

But what about the ones who do know? The ones who never took a damn thing for granted? Who tried their hardest to hold on, yet could only look on helplessly while they lost the thing they loved the most?

Isn't it so much worse for them?

79 **First Love**

Before I fell
in love with words
with setting skies
and singing birds—
it was you I fell
in love with first

80 **Her Time**

She has been feeling it for a while—that sense of awakening. There is a gentle rage simmering inside her, and it is getting stronger by the day. She will hold it close to her—she will nurture it and let it grow. She won't let anyone take it away from her. It is her rocket fuel and finally, she is going places. She can feel it down to her very core—this is her time. She will not only climb mountains—she will move them too.

81 Some Time Out

The time may not
be prime for us
though you are
a special person

We may be just
two different clocks
that do not tock
in unison

82 **Remember This**

It is impossible to know whether you truly want something until the moment it slips into the cold, hard reality of your life.

83 **In the End**

I was ready to give it all up—everything. I was half out of my mind with love. And I didn't think twice about what I was throwing into the fire, as long as I could keep it burning for just another minute—if only I was allowed to sit awhile longer beside its pale glow.

That was how I loved you in the end. With my body cold and shuddering. With empty hands over smoldering ash, counting out the minutes.

84 **How We Began**

It was how we began. Your mouth against mine, your fingers tracing along the back of my neck. You asked me to imagine what it must have been like, for the first two people who fell in love; before the word *love* was conceived. You said it felt like that for you. Like we existed in a time before love—as though we were waiting for the word to catch up to the feeling.

85 **Lover's Paradox**

Tell me that story again—the one where the world ends how it began with a boy who loves a girl and a girl who loves a boy. And she is deaf and he is blind and he tells her he loves her over and over and she writes him every day but never hears a thing back.

86 **He and I**

When words run dry
he does not try
nor do I

We are on par

He just is
I just am
and we just are

87 **Twice as Much**

I have mourned you every day
for every picture torn from my shelf
Since the wind had carried you away
I find I think of little else

I have mourned the words we spoke
the mouth you pressed into my back
the autumn leaves that fell and fell—
and left a girl in winter black

All these years—still I can't forget
the face my hands no longer touch
And the wretched day you leave this world—
I will mourn you twice as much

88 **When It's Over**

There is a point in every relationship when you realize it's over and seldom is it the day you break up. For some, that moment is long after you say goodbye. For others, the moment is long before.

89 Springtime

Morning light, leafy Sunday
the sun comes pouring in
I rouse from you a waking smile
so my day can begin

Down the street for a coffee
I stop to pick up the news
I stop for milk and flowers
And take them home to you

Do you know that cherries
have come into season?
The air feels light and warm
perhaps you are the reason

You greet me by the doorway
birdsong fills the room—
my love, look out the window
our garden's come into bloom

90 **I'm Sorry**

To the poem I put
into a book
before it was ready
I'm sorry I didn't wait
a few lines longer

To the flowers
I picked before
they were ready
When sunlight
still shone
like a prayer
on their petals
I'm sorry

To the man I will
love and love
until the word love
no longer means
anything to anyone
I'm sorry I wasn't ready

91 **A Way Out**

Do you know what it is like
to lie in bed awake
with thoughts to haunt
you every night
of all your past mistakes

Knowing sleep will set it right—
if you were not to wake

92 **The Nature of Love**

If I could tell my younger self one thing, it would be this:

There are many things in life you can postpone, but love isn't one of them.

93 **Faith**

I whisper your name like a prayer—with all the hope of heaven.

I trace the lines of your palm and draw a map to salvation.

I hear the knock of your heart and I answer it like my calling.

94 **Thirty-Three Locks**

Ten years ago, I arrived here
to this idle, halcyon town
this little seaside house

There are six doors
and fourteen windows
There are thirty-three locks
I turn them over in my head
when I can't sleep at night
I get out of bed to
press my face against
the tempered glass

Once I lived in a room
without a window
I bet you could still see
the places I wore the paint
thin with my fingernails
I still think about it sometimes
Some nights my mind
feels just like that room

95 **For Herself**

How do I thank my mother
for giving me the life
she desperately wanted
for herself?

96 **Dearer Than You Were**

If I could talk to you without the pain of our past, subtract all the hurt that came between us and left only what was good—speak the words that ring the most true—I would say

you are dearer to me now than when you were here

and I would say

you are the only person I have loved in such a fierce and uninhibited way

and I would say

I haven't forgotten you after all these years

and if I was given the choice again—I'd stay.

97 **Love Poetry**

What we once knew as conversation
we now know as poetry

When once we made love with our words
we now make words with our love

98 **The Longest Goodbye**

The longest goodbye is always the hardest. Love for the sake of love is the most painful of all protraction.

99 **Clocks**

Here in time
you are mine
my heart has not
sung louder

I do not know
why I love you so—
the clock knows not
its hour

Yet it is clear
to all that's here
that time is told
by seeing

Even though
clocks do not know
it is the reason
for their being

100 **Parallel Lines**

And I can already picture us ten years from now, living our lives like parallel lines. Looking across at each other from time to time.

101 **Souls**

When two souls fall in love, there is nothing else but the yearning to be close to the other. The presence that is felt through a hand held, a voice heard, or a smile seen.

Souls do not have calendars or clocks, nor do they understand the notion of time or distance. They only know it feels right to be with one another.

This is the reason why you miss someone so much when they are not there—even if they are only in the next room. Your soul only feels their absence—it doesn't realize the separation is temporary.

⌇

Can I ask you something?
Anything.
Why is it every time we say good night, it feels like goodbye?

102 **The Word Love**

A man with no just reason
spawned this criticism against me:

A poem should never contain the word love

I thought of this word—my word; how I wield it
like a wound, my pen dipping into its rosy-red hue
straining with want, just like my heart

I thought of my quiet, unassuming way with language
my easy intimacy with words; placing each syllable
with plain deliberation, like a vase of cut flowers

I could say a myriad of things about this man
and the myth he has perpetuated about me
others echoing his sentiment with dumb relish
and yet I know my words will be wasted on them

but I hope on you—they will bloom and flower
into poems of your own, and someday there will be
a word with which your name is synonymous

103 **A Postcard**

To the man I love, to my future.

The first time I felt your presence, I began joining the dots in the sky, wondering when our stars would align.

I often think of where you are and if you're happy. Are you in love? I hope she is gentle. I know you and I are the same in that way—we bruise a little more easily than most. You see, our souls were made in the same breath.

I know I'm running late—I'm sorry. Things haven't worked out the way I planned. But believe me when I tell you I am on my way.

Until then, think of me, dream of me and I will do the same. One day I will learn your name, and I will write it somewhere on this page. And we will realize that we have known each other all along.

104 Sound

In the sensory landscape of my life
touch came first, everything after
My mother's breath featherlight

And then there was scent
and then there was sight

The rest of my life—a silent night
Until my name found on his lips—took flight
and then there was sound

105 **Self-Preservation**

I used to think love had no limits—but I draw the line at myself.

106 **Wonder**

The first thing you sent me were fireworks. Sparks of light and color over a bridge to nowhere. I was already in love when we met that summer; I belonged to someone else. To make room for you, I had to ask the world for permission, but every answer was a dead end. But who am I to blame them for telling me what I already knew? So, I danced around you like a storm, white light against the cool black sky, like strobe lights flickering on and off. I said we could be something, you and me. I said so much and meant it, but never proved it to you, did I? We both know what my word was worth, you and me both. You took my hand under a Ferris wheel, spitting light, spinning lies. You dazzled me, you know. You were incandescent. I don't think we could have been anything, not really. But isn't it something to wonder?

107 **Whole Again**

I have moved so far away from you that I have become a myth; a lie you tell yourself each night. I am the one true thing you've held in the palm of your hand, the key to everything you wanted.

Your name smiles at me from a crumpled envelope, addressed to the past. Unsent and unseen. Inside I wrote you a story about the moon, how night after night the darkness carved at the pale curve of her body until she became half the woman she was.

There is a word that hurts my heart—one I don't ever say out loud. Like the shadow that lingers in the light, I can't separate myself from your memory. But there are some nights when I look up at the sky, and the moon is whole again.

108 **Always**

You were you
and I was I
we were two
before our time

I was yours
before I knew
and you have always
been mine too

109 Birthdays

It is a ceremony, the blowing of candles, the cutting of a cake—the mess of cream and sponge in your mouth. The taste is sweet and familiar, like a newly formed wish, fashioned from all the ones you've made before.

You don't remember them in sequence—the things you've asked for. You only recall those you wanted the most. Like the pair of neon pink roller skates you saw in the shop window when you were twelve. How deeply you felt their absence when you sat among the litter of torn wrapping paper and empty new possessions.

Or the year you turned sixteen; when your best friend's mother got really sick, and all you wanted was for her to be okay again. It was the year you learned that shooting stars were either a blessing or a curse, depending on what you wanted to believe.

Then there was that year you fell in love. The one where there weren't any candles—just you walking late at night through the city streets with your heart in pieces, wanting to give yourself to the first stranger who called you beautiful.

Since then, it's been the same every year. As soon as the first match is struck, the smell of burning takes you backward through your memory. It stops you right at that moment on that warm September night, as you watched the first trickle of melting wax hit the icing, and you couldn't think of a single damn thing you wanted—because he was standing there, in the flickering light, asking you to make a wish.

110 **A Long Time Ago**

Everything feels sentimental these days, every song feels loaded, feels somehow directed at me. Every emotion is heightened tenfold, your fingertips leaving burn marks on my skin. I think it only feels this way for me when things are beginning or when they're ending. And my love, we started this a long time ago.

111 **If You Didn't**

If you didn't know me
you would see me as they do
believe the lies they tell
about me were true

If you didn't know me
you wouldn't want to know me—
I would never be
the one for you

And you wouldn't be sorry
for missing what you never knew
If you didn't know me—
only, my love, you do

112 **Seasons**

If you were to choose a season, which would it be?
The golden dunes of summer, wild and free
The quiet breath of winter—trees bare and stark
Or spring's flowers and her honeybees?

Would you swim in the ocean or walk in the park?
Or catch the sunset before it grows dark?
What page of the calendar would you mark?
I'd choose fall—the season you came back to me

113 **Thoughts on Letting Go**

It's possible to move on from someone even if your heart refuses to let go. And it's not something you need to consciously do. It will just happen gradually, over time. The ache will always be there, but the intensity will fade, and you'll find other beautiful things to fill your days with.

114 **Who You Love**

The life you always thought you wanted before you knew any different. The sea change you didn't see coming, the sweeping vistas and cotton candy sunsets.

The meeting point between how you imagined it would be and how it has transpired. The willingness to take a chance on something that could take you somewhere new.

The dream you chose to give up on, or the one that you were coaxed into following. Who you love and who loves you back determines so much in your life.

115 **In Two Parts**

You come and go so easily
your life is as you knew—
while mine is split in two

How I envy so the half of me
who lived before love's due
who was yet to know of you

116 **Love Lost**

There is one whom you belong to
whose love—there is no song for
And though you know it's wrongful
there is someone else you long for

Your heart was once a vessel
it was filled up to the brim
until the day he left you
now everything sings of him

Of the two who came to love you
to one, your heart you gave
He lives in the stars above you—
in the love who came and stayed

117 **Stowaway**

I love the way he looks at me. Shy and half-cocked as though he is caught off guard, like he is retracing his steps to remember all the ways to make me smile. He brings me flowers every Sunday and tells me stories about mermaids and sirens with their sharp claws and beguiling lips. He says I remind him of the sea and attaches me to a metaphor I've never heard before, when I thought I had heard them all. I think someone broke his heart once and now he can't bear to be away from the ocean. He said it's strange how the smallest things can wreck a ship. Like a rock, or a wave, or a hairline crack in the hull. He calls me his little stowaway and he says it sadly, tenderly, as though I can sink him.

118 **The Last Time**

When was the last time you said I love you and meant it. When was the last time you heard those words back.

When was the last time you felt like someone knew you and not the person you've been pretending to be. When was the last time you felt like yourself.

When was the last time you heard someone say his name. When was the last time it killed you to hear it.

When was the last time you felt love well up in you like a newly struck spring. Like an outpouring of the soul.

When was the last time he called you beautiful. When was the first.

119 Set Free

Did you destroy my life
or did you set me free?

I used to think it was the first
Hindsight has shown me
it was the latter

120 **Meant to Be**

If they were meant to be in your life, nothing could ever make them leave. If they weren't, nothing in the world could make them stay.

121 **New Beginnings**

If I have learned anything this year, it's that I won't ever be ready for what life throws at me. I will never be adequately prepared. I won't have the right words when it counts for something. I won't know the right answer when fate itself is staring me down.

I've learned I can go on waiting for something, sustained by hope and nothing more, or I can put it to one side and shrug my shoulders. Bravely accept the fact that I can't keep my heart safe any more than I can stop love from taking everything from me.

I have learned to stop saying yes when I don't mean it—to live as authentically as I know how. To allow the tips of my fingers to skirt the darkness, as long as I remember to keep my eyes fixed on the light. And as one door opens and another closes, I will move forward with the knowledge that unlike so many others, I have another year ahead of me—another shot at making it all the way around the sun, and a chance to get it right this time 'round.

122 **Reasons**

I wish I knew why he left. What his reasons were. Why he changed his mind.

For all these years, I have turned it over in my head—all the possibilities—yet none of them make any sense.

And then I think, perhaps it was because he never loved me.

But that makes the least sense of all.

123 **For You**

Here are the things I want for you.

I want you to be happy. I want someone else to know the warmth of your smile, to feel the way I did when I was in your presence.

I want you to know how happy you once made me and though you really did hurt me, in the end, I was better for it.

I don't know if what we had was love, but if it wasn't, I hope never to fall in love. Because of you, I know I am too fragile to bear it.

I want you to remember my lips beneath your fingers and how you told me things you never told another soul. I want you to know that I have kept sacred, everything you had entrusted in me and I always will.

Finally, I want you to know how sorry I am for pushing you away when I had only meant to bring you closer. And if I ever felt like home to you, it was because you were safe with me. I want you to know that most of all.

124 **Motherhood**

Your name is the second one
your mother gave you
Love was the first

125 **The Age of Love**

People ask me how old I am, and I smile. It is impolite to ask a woman her age. But I don't mind at all. I tell them I am merely growing into my skin, that I have always been an old soul, and they ask me, *Doesn't your soul remain the age you were when you first fell in love?*

Well, I answer, love is older than time, and then I tell them about you—and how I have loved you for a very, very long time.

126 **Too Close**

I live my life between being loved
or being known
wishing the two were one

To be loved is a wave rushing past
the shoreline; filling every void

To be known is an ache
that never goes away

Now that you love me, are you afraid
to know me? Will distance tell you
what your heart refuses to see?

You're too close to me, my love
You're missing everything

127 **All This Love**

I don't know where it comes from, all this love I have for you. I don't know where to put it now that you're gone.

128 **My Other Self**

I met a girl today who was like me, yet so much more than I was. And she showed me who I could have been if only I had found the courage. If I had learned to say no when the question was ripe, when it was still mine to answer. If I had walked away when I knew it was the right thing to do and then kept walking.

The girl and I—we were a mirror. She, standing where I've always imagined I would be. And I—in the place she swore to herself she would never end up.

129 **One Thing**

She looked up at the sky and whispered, take anything away from me, take it all if you want to; but please—please just let me keep this one thing.

130 **More a Poet**

I fell asleep to the rain last night
And the sun came to me in a dream
Beaming down on me, sweeter than anything
More real to me than skin

A voice I knew as yours said to me
One day I woke up and with every breath
I thought of you

And I wanted to tell you
I thought of you too. You said
Nothing went wrong with us; we just let go
But you and I—we are eternal—okay?

By the time my eyes fluttered open
It was already daylight. And I found myself
Drenched in poetry. That morning I was
more a poet than I had ever been
Outside my window, it had been raining forever
And then the sun came quietly back

131 **Regrets**

There it is, that one thing in your past you wish you could undo. It sits in your mind like a big, red, tantalizing bow. A gentle tug is all it would take to set things right.

If only you could get to it.

But you can't.

132 **Wolves**

Who will protect me with you gone? Who will keep the wolves from the door while I sleep? My love, you are my shelter, my strength, my shield. Before you, I have held my own, I am a force in my own right. But you are my superpower. And now I have known life with you, how can I ever be without?

133 **Sahara**

And the weather was so damn sick of being predictable; I heard it began snowing in the Sahara and I wanted to tell you that I've changed.

134 **Only So Much**

There is only so much you can say about a man who hurts you so covertly, so gradually. The tiny paper cuts that come one after another, so measured and subdued. It barely hurts, until it does. Yet your pain is visible to no one, sometimes, not even to yourself. There is no blood to mop up, no broken glass to sweep. Not a trace of anything untoward until it gets too much, and suddenly you are a wild animal thrashing, baring your teeth, and when they ask you why, you have nothing to show, no answer to give.

135 **Like Hope**

Everything that eludes me comes close enough for me to feel the weight of it in my hands. To trace the shape of it with my fingers, to give it a name. Nothing hurts like hope. To know I have caressed the tenuous edge of my desire, coaxed it gently from the shadows, drawn it ever so slowly into my body, and then like breath, let go.

136 **Distance**

It was all I wanted for the longest time—to open my eyes and see you there. To stretch out my hand and touch the soft, yielding warmth of your skin. But now I have learned the secret of distance. Now I know being close to you was never about the proximity.

137 **Three Questions**

What was it like to love him? asked Gratitude.
It was like being exhumed, I answered. And brought to life in a flash of brilliance.

What was it like to be loved in return? asked Joy.
It was like being seen after a perpetual darkness, I replied. To be heard after a lifetime of silence.

What was it like to lose him? asked Sorrow.
There was a long pause before I responded:

It was like hearing every goodbye ever said to me—said all at once.

138 **The Keeper**

You were like a dream
I wish I hadn't
slept through

Within it I fell deeper
than your heart would
care to let you

I thought you were a keeper
I wish I could
have kept you

139 **Young Love**

Screeching tires, a near miss. A horn blaring sharply into the night. I close my eyes. Here come the flashbacks. We were losing track of the days and nights, counting fireflies and waiting for the sun to come around. I was so addicted to you. I remember the exquisite fatigue as I fought off sleep for another hit—another line of conversation. We drove down freeways and winding roads, in a sleepless stupor, the stereo blasting love songs that were a cheap imitation of what we were feeling. Sometimes I wished you would take us over the edge, and we would be forever young and crazy in love. Go slow around those curves. I only want you safe now. It doesn't matter if we're together or apart. I love you so much. I'll love you, right until the end.

140 Sad Things

Why do you write sad things? he asked. When I am here, when I love you.

Because someday, in one way or another, you will be taken from me or I you. It is inevitable. But please understand; from the moment I met you, I stopped writing for the past. I no longer write for the present. When I write sad things, I am writing for the future.

141 **The Most**

You may not know
the reason why
for a time
I wasn't I

There was a man
who came and went
on him every breath
was spent

I'm sorry I forgot
all else—
it was the most
I ever felt

142 My Place in the Universe

I feel my life culminating to a point, the delicate threads of my existence joining to form a tapestry. The events up until the present that had seemed of no particular significance, now imbued with a deeper, darker meaning.

I can see it so clearly—the greater plan. I understand that I am both the architect and tenant of my destruction. I can feel it so acutely like an ache in my chest, knowing ultimately that I am locked into a chain of events that I cannot stop, an outcome I cannot alter, feeling at once helpless yet hopelessly awed by the part I will play in this beautiful, brutal expression of the Universe.

143 **Wishing Well**

Into a well
a girl threw a penny

What do you wish for
asked the well

I wish for a penny
said the girl

144 **Losing You**

I used to think I couldn't go a day without your smile. Without telling you things and hearing your voice back. Then, that day arrived, and it was so damn hard but the next was harder. I knew with a sinking feeling it was going to get worse, and I wasn't going to be okay for a very long time.

Because losing someone isn't an occasion or an event. It doesn't just happen once. It happens over and over. I lose you every time I pick up your favorite coffee mug; whenever that one song plays on the radio, or when I discover your old T-shirt at the bottom of my laundry pile.

I lose you every time I think of kissing you, holding you, or wanting you. I go to bed at night and lose you, when I wish I could tell you about my day. And in the morning, when I wake and reach for the empty space across the sheets, I begin to lose you all over again.

145 **In Love**

You've not yet had your heart in halves
so little do you know of love—
to tell me I will soon forget
there will be others to regret

Now all the years have proved you wrong
my love for him burns bright and strong
you can't divide the stars from night—
from love there can be no respite

146 **More Than Enough**

People will do all they can to reduce you, make you lesser than you are. But you have more than enough light, more than enough goodness to spare. They can take as much as they want, but it would be akin to scooping cupfuls of the ocean from someone like you. So, let them do their best and know despite all their efforts, they remain so impossibly, so laughably small.

147 **Collision**

Do you think I have slipped into a time warp?

It was your opening line. I didn't know it then, but my past, present, and future were set to collide.

At the time, the collision felt like a gentle wake-up call. Like a lazy Sunday morning spent gently parting ways with sleep. But now when I look back, I see it for what it was—alarm bells blaring at five a.m. and a plane I couldn't miss.

I got lost in the day-to-day. I passed by prophets on the city streets with their signs, warning me about the apocalypse. I never imagined it was walking right beside me, holding my hand. Night after night, I looked into your eyes but never once did they offer me a prelude to the destruction.

Life went on without you. Of course, it did. Of course, it does. It was just an ending, they tell me, not the end.

148 **Always with Me**

Your love I once surrendered
has never left my mind

My heart is just as tender
as the day I called you mine

I did not take you with me
but you were never left behind

149 **Twenty-Seven**

What age are you when you dream about yourself. In the thick, underwater flashes of coherence not knowing you're asleep.

I am twenty-seven and the drawer has just slammed shut on my hand. And I have yet to know pain—raw and undulating—I have yet to know loss, the kind that strips you back from yourself, makes you over into something else.

In my dreams, there are photographs of me that don't exist. And I am backlit against the sun, face in shadow, hair bathed in golden light. The fabric of my subconscious looks for you, calls to you, a fisherman and his net, coming up empty. And you wear the face of someone I loved at twenty-seven. And my heart is like the ocean, breaking like waves, breaking all throughout the ages.

150 **Aftermath**

I want to talk about the aftermath of love
not the honeymoon or the hitherto
but the upshot and the convalescence
the slow, hard hauling—the heavy tow

I want to tell you about those evenings
that crept inside like a vagrant cat
and cast around its drawn-out shadow
untoward—insufferably black

I want to write about the mornings
the sterility of the stark, cold light
struck against a pair of bare shoulders
the lurid whisper of a misspent night

I want to convey the afternoon setting
the water torture of the sink
drip by drip, the clock and its ticking
and too much time left now to think

151 **A Dream of Hope**

Last night I slept for the first time since
you left and I dreamt about two suns
in an apocalyptic sky, one edged in
black and smoldering, like a cigarette burn

I saw the sea rise up so high outside
the window of my mother's old house
so I climbed up onto the tin roof
to look inside the mouth of Neptune

In a hotel room where we couldn't figure
out the light switches, my legs were
wrapped around you and I was humming
a tune that we both knew by heart

There was a woman who made a shrine
for her dead lover in the hollow of a tree
She looked straight at me with eyes
milky white and whispered, it's not too late

152 **Eden**

I will grow this love without you here
Tend to it like a wild, unkempt garden
Wait for the day when you are standing before me
(as I know you will)
When I can say, look what I have kept for you
Here is Eden like I promised
Here is the red, round apple of my heart
Not once did I falter or stop believing

153 **A Dedication**

She lends her pen
to thoughts of him
that flow from it
in her solitary

For she is his poet
And he is her poetry

154 **The Saddest Thing**

There was someone I knew, a long time ago. I was so in love with him I couldn't see straight. The saddest thing is, he felt the same way about me.

It was easy in the beginning. All we had to do was laugh at the same things and love took over and did the rest. I had never felt so connected to another person.

He would always say it felt as though I was made for him. How glad he was that he had met me. We were so sure of what we felt. We should have held tight, onto that certainty.

There is never one particular reason why two people are torn apart. All these years later, I have stopped looking for answers. I know love is never a guarantee. Not when you have the rest of the world to contend with.

Sometimes you have to step back and look at these things from a new perspective. And I know loving him has taught me something about myself, it has broadened my understanding of the world. And if it has done the same for him, then it wasn't all in vain.

155 **Metamorphosis**

I am somebody else's story. The girl who served their drink, the person they pushed past on a crowded street, the one who broke their heart. I have happened in so many places, to so many people—the essence of me lives on in these nuances, these moments.

Yet never have I been bolder or brighter than I am with you. Not once have I ever felt so alive. Whatever vessel we pour ourselves into, mine is now overflowing, brimming with life. It is transcending into something new.

Hands are no longer hands. They are caresses. Mouths are no longer mouths. They are kisses. My name is no longer a name, it is a call. And love is no longer love—love is you.

156 **Leaves**

Deep in the forest among the trees
I heard the whispering of leaves
They spoke to me of letting go
and taught me all I had to know

Springtime shoots and renewal dots
branches brittle from the frost
Leaves bravely do what we refuse
New love will come to bear the loss

When time has come to pay one's dues
you mustn't be quick to count the cost
For those who hold on to what is lost
will learn there is so much more to lose

157 **The One**

I don't want you to love me because I'm good for you, because I say and do all the right things. Because I am everything you have been looking for.

I want to be the one who you didn't see coming. The one who gets under your skin. Who makes you unsteady. Who makes you question everything you have ever believed about love. Who makes you feel reckless and out of control. The one you are infuriatingly and inexplicably drawn to.

I don't want to be the one who tucks you into bed—I want to be the reason why you can't sleep at night.

158 **Pretext**

Our love—a dead star
to the world it burns brightly—
But it died long ago

159 **A Writer's Muse**

One day he will find you. He will touch you and you will feel a lifetime of indifference—of apathy melt away in a single moment. And you will ache for him. You will love him, in the way you walk a tightrope—in the way people learn to fall asleep in a war zone. You will bleed for him until the day he is gone. You will bleed for him every day after that. The time will pass and you will feel robbed— and you will grow bitter. You will ask why, but you won't get an answer. And that is when the words will come.

160 **A Study in Denial**

Even though you're a thought that keeps circling its way
back around

Even though hearing your name is like a sledgehammer
to my heart

Even though I have never once not known what I know

Every time I come to the realization that I still love you

It is as though I've just realized it for the first time.

161 Moments

That's the tragedy of growing up—knowing you'll run out of feeling something new for the first time. The sad thing is you only get so many of those moments—a handful if you're lucky—and then you spend the rest of your life turning them over in your head.

I think that's why you meant as much to me as you did, why I held on for so long. I didn't know it back then, but you were the last time I would ever feel anything new.

162 **Entwined**

There is a line
I'm yet to sever—
it goes from me
to you

There was a time
you swore forever
and I am captive
to its pull

If you were kind
you'd cut the tether—
but I must ask you
to be cruel

163 **About Love**

When I was five I asked my mother about love. She scooped me into her arms and spun me around, her laughter filling up the room. She said love was like a red, round balloon, there was a part of you that wanted to hold on to it, a part of you that longed to see it soar into the big, open sky.

At ten, I asked my mother again about love. A soft smile played on her lips when she said, love was like a drowsy kitten that came to you, unbidden, crawled into your lap and made you the center of its world.

The day I turned twenty, I dared to ask my mother one last time about love. She tucked a lock of my hair behind my ear and held my young, hopeful face between her gentle hands. Her eyes were raw with longing when she answered, love is a dormant volcano, lying in wait, biding its time.

164 **Why I Write**

I write without knowing
whom my words will find
without thinking further
than the next line

When my heart grows
too heavy to hold—I write
from the depth of my sorrow
to dizzying heights

I write without dreams
of awards or applause
but for the joy of rendering
my soul into words

To hold tight each feeling
I am blessed to have felt
I write not to be known
But to know myself

165 **All You Can Do**

The man who says sorry when he hurts you is redeemable. The one who would never make that mistake in the first place is admirable.

But the man who perpetually fails to acknowledge his wrongs—who cannot take a minor blow to his ego to soothe and assure you—all you can do with this man is walk away.

166 **All There Was**

My greatest lesson learnt
you were mine until you weren't

It was you who taught me so
the grace in letting go

The time we had was all—
there was not a moment more

167 **For the World**

I talk to you all the time, even if you can't hear me. I tell you constantly, over and over, how much I miss you and that for me, nothing has changed. I think about the days when we could say anything to each other. My heart is like a time capsule—it keeps safe the memory of you. I know it's harder with you gone than if you had never been here at all—but I wouldn't have missed it for the world.

168 **Now and Then**

I was always meant for you. With my tennis shoes and wild hair, dragging a case with a cello hidden between its velvet walls. Even then.

I was always meant for you. In my black woolen dress and sapphire studs. Between hotel rooms and standing ovations. Even now.

I was never meant for road signs with foreign names, or lovers who spoke in exotic tongues. For maps that were composed in a language I could not read and printed in a dialect I could not write.

You said I was like a bird of prey, caged by my captors and made to sing love songs to the sky. You said my sadness was like the sun, beautiful from a distance but it hurt you too much to come closer.

I was never meant for poetry. For words carved into history, like ancient runes that told the same tragic tale over and over. If any historian were to decipher the symbols hammered into stone, they would say that I was always meant for you. Even before the first mallet had struck iron, even after all civilization has crumbled into dust and the sky is set alight with a thousand exploding stars—even then.

169 To Know Him

If you want to know his heart, pay close attention to what angers him.

If you want to know his mind, listen for the words that linger in his silence.

If you want to know his soul, look at where his eyes are when you catch him smiling.

170 **Waiting**

I try to think of a word that is closest to love and the only thing that comes to mind is your name. I try to imagine what I would say if our paths ever crossed again but I keep drawing a blank.

I've forgotten what it was like to feel the sun on my skin without thinking of how it can hurt me. I've stopped throwing myself from cliffs, with my arms in the air, waiting for the splash below.

Every day, I look in the mirror and I see more and more of my mother's face staring back at me. Every day I measure the weight of my past against the present and feel the drag of what could have been.

I find a photograph of you and wonder when I'll stop hoping. I stare at the clock, with its slow methodical hands, and dread the day when I'll know it's too late.

171 **Still**

We may not be in love anymore, but you're still the only one who knows me.

172 **Composed Of**

A film is composed of a series of stills
A page is a collection of wounds
and a book is a handful of confetti

A minute counts up to sixty
and hours down to sunset
A year subtracts all its days to January

And life?

Life is like an accordion expanding out—
compressing into one long symphonic sigh

That's how I wish to be at my last breath
knowing I stretched myself as far as I could go

173 Conversations

Most people want to save the entire world. It's a lovely thought, and I'm not saying it's not a noble pursuit—but it's impossible to save everyone. You just have to pick your little corner of the world and focus your energy there. That's the only way you will ever make a difference.

But I don't know if I can make a difference. It feels like I am screaming at the top of my lungs, but no one can hear me. No one cares. How can I change anything if I'm completely powerless?

You may be powerless now, but there will be a time when you won't be. Don't you see? And that's the time for you to be loud, to tell the world about the changes you want to see, to set them in motion.

174 **Wounded**

A bruise is tender
but does not last
it leaves me as
I always was

But a wound I take
much more to heart
for a scar will always
leave its mark

And if you should ask me
which you are
my answer is—
you are a scar

175 **He Stayed**

He stayed—long enough for the winter to thaw—for the season to yield its first flower. He kept his promise to me, for as much time as it took for the sea to tire herself out, kiss the last raindrop goodbye, and send it back to the heavens. He held on and on like the morning star, marching bravely toward the inevitable, like a person drowning desperate for something to hold. He stayed long enough to make me think he would never leave.

176 **In Your Voice**

Every time I see my name, I hear it in your voice

177 **Loving You**

Loving you is like being ten years old again, scaling a tree with my eyes bright and skyward, wanting only to get higher and higher, without a thought of how I would get back down.

178 **Moving On**

Leave him, let him go. Don't be the crazy ex-girlfriend or the shoulder to cry on. You're more than just an ego boost, a story he can tell someone he's trying to impress. Just walk away with your head held high and don't give him another second of your time. I know you love him so much that every step is killing you. But this is the moment you'll always look back on as the day you put yourself first. Go and make something beautiful of your life and I promise you, one day you'll forget he was ever there.

179 **Acceptance**

There are things I miss
that I shouldn't
and those I don't
that I should

Sometimes we want
what we couldn't—
sometimes we love
who we could

180 **Shooting Stars**

I want to light a spark tonight, without striking up a memory of you. Please don't send me shooting stars when my mind is a loaded pistol.

181 **I Had You**

Last night I had a dream that felt like a memory. A glimpse of what could have been. Crossed signals from another life.

Where instead of all this, I had you.

And life was exquisitely simple.

And we were desperately happy.

182 **Within My Reach**

I wish the love
I have come to meet
was not an inch
within my reach

I wish the prize
was so far-flung
that I would not cry
if it were not won

I wish the dream
was placed so high
that my panicked heart—
would dare not try

183 **A Love Letter to Myself**

Write love letters to yourself all the time
leave them in places you can find
Somewhere, in another time
when you will know yourself as only you can

Now tell me did it all go to plan
Did you give it all up for a man
or did you give him up for the only version
of yourself that you allowed—are you proud?

God only knows you can't have it all
this life was only meant to go in one direction
And you, with your degrees of perfection
In that small town, you've always wanted more
than anyone else around

Where did that get you in the end
A shopping list you tick off again and again
A house, a car, someone to help the days go by
It all goes by in the blink of an eye
and suddenly you are holding nothing

But don't despair—it was all worthwhile
You've put yourself first, that counts for something
For a while, it was worth everything
For a time, it was your time, and you—
you shone brighter than anyone you knew
It's more than anyone could hope—you know

I hope you do

184 **When I'm Happy**

That's the thing about happiness. It doesn't require justification. When I'm happy, I'm happy. I don't feel the need to write about it.

185 **Who You Are**

He has you, words tangled, wings clipped, folded at your breast. Trapped within yourself thinking, how did I get here? With all your promise and intellect, how did I get here? Whittled down like this, reduced to something you swore you'd never be. Now, how do you tear yourself away from him without ripping your life to shreds? You no longer recognize yourself, but sweet girl, that means you still know who you are. And while there is still a glimmer of hope behind those sad, tired eyes, know he hasn't worn you down. And while there is an ounce of fight left in you, know he hasn't won just yet. And while there is a chance in hell you get out of this, you come out swinging.

186 Your Loss

The pain you feel
you say I've caused—
but what is mine
was never yours

The truth is plain
but you refuse to see
He was lost to you
before he found me

Yet still you choose
to wage this war—
you would gladly lose it all
if it meant my loss was more

187 **Patience**

Patience and Love agreed to meet at a set time and place; beneath the twenty-third tree in the olive orchard. Patience arrived promptly and waited. She checked her watch every so often but still, there was no sign of Love.

Was it the twenty-third tree or the fifty-sixth? She wondered and decided to check, just in case. As she made her way over to the fifty-sixth tree, Love arrived at twenty-three, where Patience was noticeably absent.

Love waited and waited before deciding he must have the wrong tree and perhaps it was another where they were supposed to meet.

Meanwhile, Patience had arrived at the fifty-sixth tree, where Love was still nowhere to be seen.

Both begin to drift aimlessly around the olive orchard, almost meeting but never do.

Finally, Patience, who was feeling lost and resigned, found herself beneath the same tree where she began. She stood there for barely a minute when there was a tap on her shoulder.

It was Love.

∽

Where are you? she asked. I have been searching all my life. Stop looking for me, Love replied, and I will find you.

188 **The Night**

It's been awhile since words have found me
the time between—you'll come and go
I'd grown to love the sun around me
I've been a stranger to my woe

It's been so long since there was silence
all around me, your voice had rung
like a bird who sings to greet the morning
to tell you that the day has come

It's been some time since I've felt lonely
like a book that is no longer read
the darkness lingers on without you
it fills my empty heart with dread

It seems an age ago, since you have left me
time has filled me, with words unsaid
as the sadness seeps into me slowly
and I am left to face the night ahead

189 How Much Love

How much love is a person capable of giving? I thought
I knew the answer until I met you.

190 **A Love Story**

Beyond the shores of melancholy
there was a time I held your hand
My heart now bears an untold story
like a ship at sea, that longs for land

A great untruth, my lips have borrowed
a boundless treasure to line my chest
the wealth of words are in their sorrow—
and words are all I can bequest

We will remain unwritten throughout history
no X will mark us on the map
but in books of prose and poetry
you loved me once, in a paragraph

And your love has left me, on this island
it has filled my cup up to the brink
yet I grow thirsty in this silence—
there is not a drop for me to drink

191 **Anywhere**

It is a fallacy to believe we must always live in the present. As though we are wasting away our lives by being anywhere else. Live anywhere you damn well want. Sometimes the past calls to you because it has something to say. Your future may have some crucial gem of knowledge to impart. Our lives are not linear, even if our bodies are fixed to a moment. Our minds can travel back and forth at will. The greatest trick in the world is time. All that existed before still remains, as sure and real as everything still to come.

192 **Stardust**

If you came to me with a face I have not seen, with a voice I have never heard, I would still know you. Even if centuries separated us, I would still feel you. Somewhere between the sand and the stardust, through every collapse and creation, there is a pulse that echoes of you and I.

When we leave this world, we give up all our possessions and our memories. Love is the only thing we take with us. It is all we carry from one life to the next.

193 **Again**

You will come back to me many times over
as a flower
a white cat
the king of hearts in a deck

You will come to me
as love
as a symbol of it
as a lover I'll regret
or a dear friend I knew I'd wronged

You will come back to me
as a lesson
a song
a star-shaped birthmark
on the cheek of a beautiful stranger

You will come back to me again and again
in your shape-shifter clothes and you'll hold
your breath and wait for me to see through
your disguise, to catch you out and smile
your secret back at you knowing, like the sun

you'll always come back
in a multitude of miracles
you'll always come back
like the memory of September
you'll always come back
but never, never again as yourself

194 **Gone**

The sad thing is, the moment you start to miss someone, it means they're already gone.

195 The Butterfly Effect

Close your eyes and think about that boy. Tell me how he makes you feel. Let your mind trace over his tired shoulders. Allow your thoughts to linger on that beautiful smile. Take a deep breath and try to put those dark thoughts aside. For once let go of the reins you've wrapped so tightly around your heart. I know you are scared. Who could blame you? Love is a hurricane wrapped inside a chrysalis. And you are a girl walking into the storm.

196 **Ingredients of a Poem**

Someone you miss
The whir of a blade
A half-checked list

A cake made to savor
Someone's misfortune
That swings in your favor

The clock on the hour
The run of the mill
Love that has soured

The close of a fist
The start of a book
Whatever you wish

197 If at All

Is love a fortress
Is it a sword
or is it something more?

They say that love
comes easily
if at all

Comes willingly
and willfully
struck out of the blue

Struck at the heart
where it had started
because of you

198 **Between Us**

There is always something between us, my love: a closed door, an endless corridor, a locked screen. There you are under the lamppost at dusk. Is it summer or are we still in spring? I can see you across the road, arms above your head waving hello. In my chest, something crashes hard as a head-on collision. And suddenly you grow further away like gravity turned on its side, you are up, and I am down. Here comes the feeling of falling I'd forgotten, tried to bury beneath the years. Do you see me anymore, my dear, do you trust yourself now? Does it make you smile to know you were right about me all along, somewhere deep down, does it kill you?

199 **Before There Was You**

When I used to look above
all I saw was sky
and every song
that I would sing
I sung not knowing why

All I thought and all I felt
was only just because
never was it ever you—
until it was all there was

200 **Her Words**

Love a girl who writes
and live her many lives
you have yet to find her
beneath her words of guise

Kiss her blue-inked fingers
forgive the pens they marked
The stain of your lips upon her—
the one she can't discard

Forget her tattered memories
or the pages others took
you are her ever after—
the hero of her book

201 **Recognition**

I've never met you before, but I recognize this feeling.

202 **Empty**

It is one of those nights where I am looking for something to console me. Where I go to places that I shouldn't. Here in this moment, I have agency—I can choose whether to stay away or get hurt. Why do I choose to get hurt? When I know I will never truly recover what I've lost. When it is clear I will only keep losing more of myself in the process. Sometimes I think of everyone I've ever loved—anyone who got close enough to claim some small part of me. And how you—my bright, shining hope—came along and took what precious little I had left.

203 **Sundays with Michael**

I hold my breath and count to ten
I stand and sit, then stand again.
I cross and then uncross my legs
the planes are flying overhead

The dial turns with every twist
around the watch, around his wrist
Resting there with pen in hand
who could ever understand?

The way he writes of all I dream
things kind yet cruel and in-between
where underneath those twisted trees
a pretty girl fallen to her knees

Who could know the world we've spun?
I shrug my shoulders and hold my tongue
I hold my breath and count to ten
I stand and sit, then stand again

204 My Heartache

If this is my heartache, then let it be mine to endure. Permit me to feel it in its entirety. Don't tell me how much of you I am allowed to love.

205 **The Girl He Loves**

There was a man who I once knew
for me there was no other
The closer to loving me he grew
the more he would grow further

I tried to love him as his friend
then to love him as his lover
but he never loved me in the end—
his heart was for another

206 **This Was the Year**

This was the year I didn't see coming—the one that shook me out of complacency. When I learned to stop being compliant, to demand what was rightfully mine, refuse to settle for anything less than what I deserved.

I lost patience with small talk, fell in love with midnight conversations. I crossed deserts and oceans with the man I love at my side, as we lived out of suitcases, drunk on life and laughter.

This was the year that came with a gentle tap on the shoulder, reminding me who I was and what I could be, if only I'd just open my arms and let the light in, stop overthinking and start living. Give myself permission to fall as long as I got back up again.

I held the ones I love closer—let go of the things that weren't meant to be mine. Looked my past dead in the eye and said, *You're not welcome here anymore.* Chased away the cobwebs that I had let linger for too long. Told the moon I was sorry, but this is now my time in the sun.

207 **In the Wrong Hands**

In the wrong hands, your past is a weapon.

208 **A Premonition**

There are some people who you look at, and you can just tell how their story will end. I don't know what it is; they have everything going for them, yet it will never be enough. But when I look at you, I just know instinctively, that despite the odds against you and although life will always find a way to test you, someday you'll have everything you want. Your ending will be a happy one.

209 **Choose Love**

My mother once said to me there are two kinds of men you'll meet. The first will give you the life you want and the second will give you the love you desire. If you're one of the lucky few, you will find both in the one person. But if you ever find yourself having to choose between the two, then always choose love.

210 **Someone Else**

I don't think it's right, telling someone to stop needing somebody else. Have you ever felt the twist of loneliness in the pit of your stomach? Sat in silence with nothing to which you could look forward? The last thing you should do is tell someone they can fix it on their own. That no one else can fix it for them. Believe me, sometimes all it takes is someone else.

211 **As Though We Knew**

As though we knew pain, and we were ready to know
it in more intricate and damning ways
to be familiar with its every shade—to know its name

It came to us in abundance and we didn't question why
one doesn't question the sky when it is always
in your line of vision

Why should it not prepare me for what's to come
when grief has struck me dumb from every direction
but I saw it coming because I knew what to look for
how to see the signs

And this pain I called it before its time, I made it mine
even before it was here, I wasn't afraid because I knew
exactly when it was due, and I could brace myself

against the shock of the inevitable,
we know it only too well
it hits harder those who are charmed, who had been kept
out of harm's way, who'd never had to live a day
like all the ones we have lived to tell

212 **My Heart**

Perhaps I never loved enough
If only I'd loved much more
I would not nearly had so much
left waiting, for you in store

If I had given away my heart—
to those who came before
it would be safer left in parts—
but now you have it all

213 **Attainment**

At the start, I only understood
the accumulation of things
the raw, pulsing desire for more

I would spend every waking moment
trapped in motion, racing toward
each new obsession that reared itself
prodigious and uninhibited

It isn't that my appetite
has reached the end of her rope
I still want everything
I have ever wanted

But since you, my life
is less about attainment
and more about holding on
to what I already have

214 **Closer to Me**

It was long ago, yet you feel closer to me than yesterday, more hopeful than tomorrow.

You are as far and near as memory.

As distant as the sun,

as close as its light on my skin.

215 **Someone Like You**

Do you think there is the possibility of you and me? In this lifetime, is that too much to hope for? There is something so delicate about this time, so fragile. And if nothing ever comes of it, at least I have known this feeling, this wonderful sense of optimism. It is something I can always keep close to me—to draw from in my darkest hour like a ray of unspent sunshine. No matter what happens next, I will always be glad to know there is someone like you in the world.

216 **Want**

What do you long for
in your heart of hearts
in this eruption of light
between eons of dark

What do you wish for
at the cut of the cake
A knife in your hand
for a love you still ache

You'll get what you want
if you're willing to wait
If not when you want it
then when it's too late

217 **In My Words**

I have buried myself so deep in my words that sometimes I can't tell if I am the person writing or the one hiding between the lines.

218 **The Poet**

Why do you write? he asked.

So I can take my love for you and give it to the world, I replied.

Because you won't take it from me.

219 **Crazy Love**

Anyone who knew me then would say I loved you far too much. Like a wildfire or the sharp edge of a knife. Anyone would have told you I stopped being the person I was the second you walked into my life. They would have said love wasn't supposed to drive you crazy, make you want to scratch at your skin. And they were right. Because there was love and then there was you.

220 **Through Me**

Have I been faithful?
Yes, my body I've kept
beating to your
melodramatic drum

But my heart—oh my heart
has wandered over to
places I didn't allow
myself to follow

And you?
I think you're so
desperate for something
that proves you are still
worthy of love

Is that the cause
for your indecision
Do you crave someone
you can impress
without trying?

Is that why, my love
is that why you are running?

You are going to her
You are going through me

221 **A Question**

It was a question I had worn on my lips for days—like a loose thread on my favorite sweater I couldn't resist pulling—despite knowing it could all unravel around me.

Do you love me? I ask.

In your hesitation I found my answer.

222 **What I Would Tell You**

To you, love was about multitudes.
To me, love was inordinate.

I love you, I would say.
How much? you would ask.

I couldn't find the words to answer you then. But they have found their way to me since. And this is what I would tell you.

I would blanket the world in utter darkness; I would pull back the veil and reveal to you a blinding crescendo of stars. I would drain all the seven seas and ask you to count—one by one—every grain of sand that clings to the ocean floor.

I would tally the beat of every human heart that has echoed since the dawn of our becoming.

And as you look in awe at the sheer magnitude of my admission, I would take your hand in mine and tell you; if only you had let me, this is how much I could have loved you.

223 Love Hurts

Do you remember what you said to me that day, long before we knew what we would be, before you whispered my name to me, raw and tender, like it hurt you to say it.

You told me you were the bravest when you're in love, so don't you dare stand there and tell me you're afraid.

224 **All the Time**

Did you find your ever after?
Is there somewhere you belong?
Is your world now filled with laughter?
Is there nothing for which you long?

Do you ever look behind you?
And wonder about what you see?
When the memories come to find you—
do you ever think of me?

Do you think that love can lessen,
if you pretend it isn't there?
Do you ever, ever question
what could have been if we dared?

Are you happy to let it linger?
Does it never cross your mind?
The world that slipped through our fingers—
I think of it all the time

225 **Pandora's Box**

Longing has a language
that is all her own
The language of skin
the language of flowers

I am a body of longing
a vessel of language

For you, I am calamity
in a locked box
where the key is still turning

For you, I am a mistress
in her ivory tower humming

For you, I am a songbird
preening her feathers

For you, for you
I am a bed of roses
blooming

226 **After You**

If I wrote it in a book
could I shelve it?

If I told of what you took
would that help it?

If I will it
can I un-feel it
now I've felt it?

227 **Thoughts**

Dawn turns to day
as stars are dispersed
wherever I lay
I think of you first

The sun has arisen
the sky, a sad blue
I quietly listen—
the wind sings of you

The thoughts we each keep
that are closest to heart
we think as we sleep—
and you're always my last

228 **Happiness**

I know my being happy is an anomaly. No one knows me better than you. But I can say without avoiding your gaze, without crossing my fingers behind my back; or the other things I do when speaking untruthfully—I am happy. I know the rain does not discriminate between day or night and either will hold its own light and dark—but now, at this very moment, I feel like I am the sun. And I know in my heart, I will always look upon this time—not without a sense of melancholy—that it was the happiest in my life.

229 **Nostalgia**

Do you remember our first day? The fog lifted and all around us were trees linking hands, like children playing.

Our first night, when you stood by the door, conflicted, as I sat there with my knees tucked under my chin and smiling.

Then rainbows arching over and the most beautiful sunsets I have ever seen.

How the wind howls as the sea whispers, I miss you.

Come back to me.

230 **Gilded Bars**

Do you believe yourself free?
Those gilded bars around you
are they not purely ornamental?
Set against a soaring blue sky
blazing and sentimental

All you knew of love was what they told you
The lies you tell yourself are what hold you
All the while your wings are itching to unfold

You see—others were here before you
who had lived and died gazing at the sky
Some made it to sea, others to blue
then there were those like me and you
girls who thought they were free
until they tried to leave

231 **Pieces of You**

He knows I can't tell a joke without laughing. And how I'm always talking about second chances. He knows I sleep all day and wake up tired. And I could never give anyone a straight answer.

I cried the first time I told him about you. I said I was sorry as he held me so close. He said he now knew why my eyes were like searchlights. How they looked at the sky with such longing. And why I read my stars in the paper each morning.

He left me one Sunday with his cup half empty. I padded downstairs and saw the writing on the wall. Outside the rain was already falling. And there were still pieces of you behind every door.

232 **A Meeting of Selves**

On a long, empty road I was walking, I met my future self. Her hair, white as snow, hung down to her hips, with eyes that carried the wisdom of a sage. She pointed at the city behind me, the one I had left crumbling into dust, and she said,

There is our past self among the ruins. She, the girlish one, the foolish one, the one who longs for a place with us here, where she is not welcome. The one who seeks to undo what we've done. She is chaos and ego. She knows only darkness and destruction.

She unfurled her fists, palms pointed in my direction.

And here you are, our present self, a woman in bloom, a picture of temperance, regard for kindness and humility. You have a strength that carries your entire life and the life of others. Knowledge of something sacred has changed and shaped you in a myriad of ways.

Then, she lifted her chin and her gaze penetrating mine, reflected the depths of her sincerity. And what you must now understand is the two of you should never be allowed to meet.

233 **I Know**

I felt the warmth of your goodbye
The emotion tangled with another
The sadness came with something other
For once I couldn't bring myself to cry

I asked for peace—a silent choir
In the growing shadow of my life
The blunting of my lover's knife
Running all this time against the wire

Here it comes, our solemn parting
Gratitude shapes my weary mouth
I've said too much again somehow
All without you ever asking

I wish I could throw up all my woes
Beat my fists against your chest
I had thought you loved me best
You had thought so too I know

234 **The Long Way**

You're the girl who takes the long way home. This is the way you do it. This way you will have stories to tell. About lovers and liars, thieves and kings. You will have spine-chilling tales to spin.

You will see the ones who rose so fast, dazzled for a moment before they crashed back down to earth, crawled back into the dust.

But not you. Never you.

This is the way you've always been. A hook at the end of a long, long line. Waiting patiently. You will get there and believe me when you get there: you will be glad you took your time.

235 **Possibility of Love**

Yes, I think it is entirely possible to fall in love with someone you've never met. Physicality is an expression of intimacy—not an indication of it.

236 **The Gift of Everything**

You were the bearer of heartache
of pain, like nothing I had ever known
But look at what I have because of you
Look at what I've built
Only now can I look back
and recognize the gift
you have given me

Only now can I look at the
all-consuming beauty of my life
press my palm to yours and say
Thank you for the gift of everything

CONTENTS

35 New Poems*

* *Numbers reflect poem number rather than page number.*

Selected Poems

Acknowledgments

Thank you to Alec Shane from Writers House. This book would not be possible without you.

Kirsty Melville for an amazing and creative partnership that has spanned nearly a decade and ten books. I hope there will be many more!

Thank you Patty, Kathy, and the team at Andrews McMeel for always cheering me on.

Al Zuckerman—working with you has been one of the greatest highlights of my career.

Michael and Ollie, thank you for the gift of everything.

About the Author

Novelist and poet Lang Leav was born in a refugee camp when her family were fleeing the Khmer Rouge regime. She spent her formative years in Sydney, Australia, in the predominantly migrant town of Cabramatta. Among her many achievements, Lang is the winner of a Qantas Spirit of Youth Award, Churchill Fellowship, and Goodreads Choice Award.

Her first book, *Love & Misadventure* (2013), was a breakout success, and her subsequent poetry books have all been international best-sellers. In 2016, Lang turned her attention to fiction, and her debut novel *Sad Girls* shot to #1 on the *Straits Times* and other best-seller charts internationally.

Lang actively participates in international writers' festivals and her tours consistently draw massive crowds. With a combined social media following of two million, Lang's message of love, loss, and female empowerment continues to resonate with her multitude of readers.

Lang has been featured on CNN, SBS Australia, Intelligence Squared UK, Radio New Zealand and in various publications, including *Vogue, Newsweek,* the *Straits Times,* the *Guardian,* and the *New York Times.* She currently resides in New Zealand with her partner and fellow author, Michael Faudet.